TOOLS FOR CAREGIVERS

- **ATOS:** 0.5
- **GRL:** B
- **WORD COUNT:** 29

- **CURRICULUM CONNECTIONS:** colors

Skills to Teach

- **HIGH-FREQUENCY WORDS:** a, are, is, our, the
- **CONTENT WORDS:** banana, bus, color, duck, hat, shirts, spider, yellow
- **PUNCTUATION:** periods
- **WORD STUDY:** long /o/, spelled ow (yellow); short /a/, spelled a (banana, hat); short /u/, spelled u (bus, duck)
- **TEXT TYPE:** information report

Before Reading Activities

- Read the title and give a simple statement of the main idea.
- Have students "walk" though the book and talk about what they see in the pictures.
- Introduce new vocabulary by having students predict the first letter and locate the word in the text.
- Discuss any unfamiliar concepts that are in the text.

After Reading Activities

Yellow is a very bright color. What other colors are bright? Explain that there are different shades and tints of each color. Tint is a mixture of color with white. This lightens the color. Shade is a mixture of a color with black. This darkens the color. Have the readers practice tinting and shading colors by adding white or black paint to other colors. What colors are they seeing?

Tadpole Books are published by Jump!, 5357 Penn Avenue South, Minneapolis, MN 55419, www.jumplibrary.com

Copyright ©2020 Jump! International copyright reserved in all countries. No part of this book may be reproduced in any form without written permission from the publisher.

Editor: Jenna Trnka **Designer:** Anna Peterson

Photo Credits: Silver Spiral Arts/Shutterstock, cover; Nataliia K/Shutterstock, 1; Efetova Anna/Shutterstock, 3 (background); Scott Hales/Dreamstime, 3 (foreground); Studio-Annika/iStock, 2ml, 4–5; Evannovostro/Shutterstock, 2mr, 6–7; stu99/iStock, 2tr, 8–9; bergamont/Shutterstock, 2tl, 10–11; Strannik9211/Dreamstime, 2br, 12–13; Sergey Novikov/Shutterstock, 2bl, 14–15; KETiKET/Shutterstock, 16 (left); Olga Vorontsova/Shutterstock, 16 (right).

Library of Congress Cataloging-in-Publication Data is available at www.loc.gov or upon request from the publisher.
ISBN: 978-1-64128-952-8 (hardcover)
ISBN: 978-1-64128-953-5 (paperback)
ISBN: 978-1-64128-954-2 (ebook)

FUN WITH COLORS

YELLOW

by Anna C. Peterson

TABLE OF CONTENTS

WORDS TO KNOW

banana

bus

duck

hat

shirts

spider

YELLOW

yellow ┈┈▶

Yellow is a color.

duck

The duck is yellow.

hat

The hat is yellow.

The bus is yellow.

The banana is yellow.

spider

The spider is yellow.

Our shirts are yellow.

LET'S REVIEW!

Look around you. What else is yellow?

INDEX